S0-CDS-689

Hang 10

Hang 10

A Collection of Surf Wisdom

RUNNING PRESS

PHILADELPHIA · LONDON

Library of Congress Cataloging-in-Publication Number 00-134988
ISBN 0-7624-0978-9

This book may be ordered by mail from the publisher.
Please include $1.00 for postage and handling.
But try your bookstore first!

Running Press Book Publishers
125 South Twenty-second Street
Philadelphia, Pennsylvania 19103-4399

Visit us on the web!
www.runningpress.com

Live to surf; surf to live.

Surfing proverb

There's an energy in the water
that gives you every kind of feeling:
peace, excitement, fear, a huge
adrenaline rush, discouragement,
and frustration.

Rochelle Ballard
Professional surfer

In the beginning, some possible names for the Beach Boys were the Surfers (which was already taken by a group from Hawaii), the Lifeguards, the Beach Bums, and the Woodies.

Surfing has come to include

both the stand-up surfer, as well as the bodyboarder. Bodyboarding has only been around for about 25 years. The difference is that a surfer lying on his or her stomach on a very short, spongelike board can ride a wave at a more intense stage called "closing out." Bodyboarders love riding through the tube formed by a wave, which is breaking across the length of the entire beach.

Surfing Slang

✦ **drown the line**—a long ride

✦ **hang ten or five**—number
of toes hanging over the nose
of the surfboard. Hang five
can sometimes be done on

a shortboard, but hang ten can
only be done on a longboard.

✦ **locked in**—standing on the
surfboard inside the wave's curl

✦ **smokin' a pipe**—tearing down
the face of a wave in the barrel

The 1963 flick, *Beach Party,* starring Frankie Avalon and Annette Funicello, was filmed at Paradise Cove in California.

There are moments when I enter the water, that I really do feel the presence of God. Particularly in Hawaii, where you're surrounded by these tremendous currents of energy, to a point where there's no denying this force greater than your own.

Aaron Chang
Photographer

I love "talking story."
Surfers sometimes take
as much pleasure from
sitting around and
talking about surfing as
they do actually surfing.

Fred Hemmings
World champion surfer

One of the most
dangerous waves
in the world is
caused by "Jaws,"
a mushroom-like reef
located in the
Hawaiian Islands.
The wave may be
taller than 50 feet.

In regards to the best
wave that she ever rode:

It was a long, long and
deep barrel. It was at
Nias, north of Sumatra,
an island in Indonesia.
It was about a four-to-six
foot swell and I could
get a set wave that was

probably five foot at least
[10-foot face]. I was
laughing all the way in.
It was epic.

Claudia Ferrari
Professional bodyboarder

According to *Guinness World Records 2000*, the biggest surfing competition is the G-Shock U.S. Open of Surfing at Huntington Beach, California.

The first surfing
movie was made by
Thomas Edison,
who filmed
some surfers at
Waikiki in 1898.

Polynesians, the first surfers, rode the Pacific Ocean on wooden boards, sometime between 1500 B.C. and 400 A.D.

World's Best Surf Spots

- **Australia:** Black Rock, The Bluff, Burleigh Heads, North Narrabeen, Shark Island

- **California:** Blacks, Lower Trestles, Malibu, Newport Wedge, Oxnard, Rincon

- **Hawaii:** Backdoor, Honolua Bay,

Maalaea, Pipeline, Pupukea, Off the Wall, Rocky Point, Sunset Beach

- ◉ **Indonesia:** Nias, Padang

- ◉ **Mexico:** Puerto Escondido

- ◉ **South Africa:** Jeffrey's Bay, Cave Rock

- ◉ **Tahiti:** Moorea

According to Jan. 1985 issue of *Surfer* magazine

"Misirlou," recorded by Dick Dale and his Del-Tones in 1962, became the title song for Quentin Tarantino's 1994 movie *Pulp Fiction.*

American women have surfed as long ago as the days of ancient Hawaii, and more recently on the mainland U.S. shores of California since the early 1920s.

Surfing is an art—we draw a new line on each wave we ride. It's also a science. You need to study the patterns of the ocean. And it's an ongoing lesson, because every few years the tides completely change.

Rochelle Ballard
Professional surfer

Today, surfing free style
tricks share many
moves with skateboarding,
such as a 360-degree
spin out of the water while
in a half-pipe.

To me, the sea is like a person—like a child that I've known a long time. It sounds crazy, I know, but when I swim in the sea I talk to it. I never feel alone when I'm out there.

Gertrude Ederle
American swimmer

Different Types of Surfers

- ❧ **goofy foot**—a surfer who stands on the board with the right foot forward

- ❧ **kook**—a rookie

- ❧ **natural foot**—a surfer who stands on the board with the left foot forward

❖ **snake or shoulder hopper**—a very rude surfer who cuts in on a rider's right of way

After World War I, Surfboards evolved from solid wood to hollow plywood and were called "toothpicks." Then they evolved from wood to plastic after World War II. Surfboards became cheaper, lighter, shorter, and eventually more stable with the invention of the tri-fin.

The popular 1959 teen flick, *Gidget,* starring Sandra Dee as the title role and James Darren as Moondoggie, was based on Frederick Kohner's 1957 novel, which shares the same name. The real Gidget, Kohner's teenage daughter Kathy, got her nickname, short for "Girl Midget," from surfer Terry "Tubesteak" Tracey.

Surfing to me has a two-fold effect, it is a way to commune with nature, and it is a way to match myself against the ocean on a personal level. I go as far as I can personally, and this is satisfying to me.

Dr. Bruce Gabrielson, Ph.D.
Founder of the first officially recognized
U.S. High School Surfing League

Only the drummer of the Beach Boys, Dennis Wilson, actually surfed.

Once more upon the waters!
yet once more!
And the waves bound
beneath me as a steed
That knows his rider.

Lord Byron (1788–1824)
English poet

Never turn your back on the ocean — Mother Nature. You never know when she'll come through to get you. No one is king of the ocean.

Darryl "Flea" Virostko
Professional bodyboarder

48

A Board Primer

A **shortboard** ranges from 5 feet 6 inches to 6 feet 11 inches in length. It also has a tri-fin setup.

There are two types of **longboards**: a mini log, or a short longboard, which ranges from 7 feet 10 inches to 8 feet 6 inches and the modern version which varies from 8 feet 6 inches to 11 feet in length.

Longboards became less fashionable in the 1960s through the 1970s but they are slowly regaining popularity. Modern longboards typically have a single fin.

In order to ride waves, which range from 10 to 30 feet, one uses a board called a **gun**. It is the same length as a longboard, but it has a pin–shaped nose and tail.

There is a wide range of fin and board styles.

Dick Dale recorded
original material
for Disneyland's
Space Mountain
roller coaster ride.

The rising popularity of surfing by women is due to professional women surfers who push the sport to new limits and to the small, lightweight twin-fin board.

The sea speaks a
language polite
people never repeat.
It is a colossal
scavenger slang
and has no respect.

Carl Sandburg (1878–1967)
American poet

Surfing holds a heavy mystique for those who aren't a part of it. We're drawn to it because we all want to be surfers deep down, but we know we can't be.

Haysun Hahn
Former President of Bureau de Style,
a trend forecasting company

More Surfing Slang

* **cranking**—awesome surf

* **ripe**—perfect for surfing, as in a wave

* **ripping**—surfing very well, as if one is "ripping the wave to shreds"

* **stoked**—excited, especially due to a ride on an awesome wave

The 1966 film *The Endless Summer* inspired audiences to continue their quest for the "elusive perfect wave."

Duke Paoa Kahanamoku, "The Father of Modern Surfing," introduced a ten-foot board in 1910.

In regards to why people surf:

To feel the energy of the living ocean and salt water on the skin. To experience harmony in motion with nature and be challenged physically and mentally by the dynamic changes of each swell.

Shannon McIntyre
Surfboard shaper

He is a Mercury
—a brown mercury.
His heels are winged,
and in them is the
swiftness of the sea.

Jack London (1876–1967)
American writer and amateur surfer

John Severson's 1978 film *Big Wednesday* acquired its title from the director's observation that "all the big days" on Hawaii seemed to be Wednesdays. Thus, the final scene was shot at Waimea Bay on a Wednesday.

I fell on my face on the wall of the wave and went over backwards. I hit the bottom so hard, it was like a car crash; it was that intense. I thought I'd broken my back. I just went numb and buckled.

Taj Burrow
Professional surfer

Three Hawaiian students introduced surfing to mainland U.S. in Northern California in 1885.

Most World Professional Series Surfing Titles

✳ American Kelly Slater won the men's title 6 times, in 1992 and from 1994 to 1998.

✳ The women's title is held by 3 women, who each won 4 times:

American Frieda Zamba (1984 to 1986 and 1988), Australian and former South African surfer Wendy Botha (1987, 1989, 1991, and 1992), and Australian Lisa Anderson (1993 to 1996).

According to *Guinness World Records 2000*

When you go out there (to surf), go hard (and) rip it.

Claudia Ferrari
Professional bodyboarder

Australia's first surfer
was Isabel Letham
who rode tandem with
Duke Paoa Kahanamoku,
or on his shoulders,
in the summer of 1915.

Best U.S. Surf Locations on the East Coast

* **Florida:** Sebastian Inlet

* **New York:** Montauk Point

* **North Carolina:** Cape Hatteras

**According to Doug Werner,
author of *Surfer's Start-Up: A Beginner's
Guide to Surfing (Second Edition)***

Surfing is a lifestyle.
Being a part of the ocean,
having the freedom to
play on the beach in
the sun, wearing bathing
suits, being with your
friends—all that good
stuff gets carried through
in the sport of surfing.

Rochelle Ballard
Professional surfer

I could not help concluding
that this man felt the most
supreme pleasure while
he was driven on so fast
and so smoothly by the sea.

Captain James Cook (1728–1779)
British explorer

Originally, Hawaiian boards lacked fins until Tom Blake put one on his surf-board.

Wave Lingo

- **bomb**—a huge wave which suddenly appears

- **monolith or monster**—a gigantic wave

- **tube, pipe, glasshouse, barrel, bowl,** or **shacks**—a hollow, tube-like piece of the wave

I definitely do not think
that "women's surfing"
is any more of a trend than
"men's surfing." The act
of surfing is too much of
an addiction to be a passing
phase in anyone's life.

Shannon McIntyre
Surfboard shaper

Jack London's surfing experiences served as the basis for a chapter in *The Cruise of the Snark.* His writing helped spark Americans' interest in surfing.

A big part of my success
has been wave knowledge.
I feel like I've done
well at Pipeline more than
anywhere else
because I know the wave.

Kelly Slater
World champion surfer

Surfing Movies

- *Gidget* (1959)
- *The Endless Summer* (1966)
- *Big Wednesday* (1978)
- *North Shore* (1987)
- *Point Break* (1991)
- *The Endless Summer II* (1994)

Movies
with
Surfing

- *Dark Star* (1974)

- *Apocalypse Now* (1979)

The mantra of big wave wipeouts is "relax" and save oxygen until the force of the wave subsides enough to move towards safety. There are times in life when you stop fighting in order to survive.

Fred Hemmings
World champion surfer

Surfing was not just a Hawaiian pastime. Riding on wooden planks was also popular in the late 1830s off the coast in west Africa.

My best all-time song is

"Wipe Out" by the Surfaris.

When I used to take

off on big waves at Sunset

Beach, this tune was

in my head many times.

Dr. Bruce Gabrielson, Ph.D.
Founder of the first officially recognized
U.S. High School Surfing League

*There are never two waves
that are exactly the same.
And you never have exactly
the same experience surfing.
Being there before and
knowing what to do plays
a big part in allowing you
to evolve and progress
and hopefully, handle your-
self in difficult situations.*

Aaron Chang
Photographer

Linda Benson, the Pacific
Coast Women's champion
from 1959 through 1961,
was a surfing double
for Deborah Walley, who
took over the role of
Gidget, in the 1961 sequel
Gidget Goes Hawaiian.

[A beginner's board] should be around 10 feet long. It is much easier to start out on a longboard; wait until you are reasonably good to switch to a shorter board.

Kelly Slater
World champion surfer

Simon Anderson
of Sydney,
Australia created
the triple fin
"thruster" to
provide more
stability.

Most World Amateur Champion Surfing Titles

- Australian Michael Novakov, won the men's title 3 times, in 1982, 1984, and 1986 in the kneeboard event.

❖ Two American women, who each won twice, hold the women's title: Joyce Hoffman (1965 and 1966) and Sharon Weber (1970 and 1972).

According to
Guinness World Records 2000

Softer materials are better in colder water and stiffer materials in warm water. As for big waves, and anything over 15 feet, I like a bigger board, and wider board, but in smaller waves I like narrow short boards.

Carol Philips
Former President of the Association
of Women Bodyboarders

Although surfing as a sport has made great strides, it will never gain the kind of recognition, influence, or support other sports have until it becomes an Olympic sport.

Dr. Bruce Gabrielson, Ph.D.
Founder of the first officially recognized
U.S. High School Surfing League

The Wave

* **curl**—the curve of a breaking wave

* **face**—the unbroken front

* **soup**—foamy, breaking water

* **wall**—unbroken, large wave

Surfing is something you can enjoy for a long time. The parameters of surfing are being pushed more and more now, with no concept of quitting. Now, because of a lot of things, the evolution of technology inside and outside the sport, plus the abundance of leisure time in our society, there's no reason to quit.

Aaron Chang
Photographer

Surfing Stuff

A **trackpad** and **surfing wax** will keep your feet stationary on the board during quick, sharp turns.

Apply the wax from the edge of the track pad towards the nose, about $\frac{2}{3}$ up the board. In the event of a wipeout, the **leash** keeps the board close by. It should match the length of the board.

Brazil has great waves to surf if you are in the right places in the right time. You'll score super nice days of surfing, and beach breaks such as, Copacabana, Itacoatiara and Pepino can give you great bodyboarding moments!

Guilherme Tamega
World champion surfer

The original title for
the Beach Boys' number
one hit, "Surf City,"
was "Surfin' Woodie."

Men generally wear board shorts and women wear full swimsuits in order to prevent their clothes from flying off during a wipeout. When the water is cool, surfers may wear rash guards underneath their wetsuits for skin irritation and extra warmth. It is also important for surfers to keep their heads, hands, and feet warm by wearing hoods, neoprene-webbed gloves, and booties in cold water.

I don't look at it like
I'm "charging" it, just that
there's a wave and
I want to ride it. I do get
a huge rush in a big wave
that is not comparable
to anything else in the world.

Carol Philips
Former President of the Association
of Women Bodyboarders

The interesting thing about surfing
is that the test of a good surfer
comes at a subconscious level—
how well you intuitively react
to situations and how quickly you
react, and how you react with
style and grace.

Aaron Chang
Photographer

If we help our sport grow, we will grow with it as well.

Claudia Ferrari
Professional bodyboarder

Surfing will always be cool, but at the same time it'll always be on the fringe.

Haysun Hahn
Former President of Bureau de Style,
a trend-forecasting agency

Out of the water I am nothing.

Duke Paoa Kahanamoku (1880–1968)
Professional surfer,
"The Father of Modern Surfing"

Photography Credits

Corbis:

© Bettmann: p. 15

© Rick Doyle: back cover, pp. 8–9, 107, 124–125

© Macduff Everton: front cover

© Hulton-Deutsch Collection: p. 115

© Douglass Peebles: p. 75

© Reuters New Media, Inc.: pp. 28–29, 49, 56–57, 65, 87, 110–111, 119

H. Armstrong Roberts:

© H. Armstrong Roberts: pp. 2, 25, 78, 96

© R. Kord: pp. 83, 92–93

© Robert Landau: pp. 41, 53

© S. Lissau: pp. 18, 36–37, 44–45, 60, 70–71

© Guy Motil: pp. 102–103

© Bill Ross: p. 33

This book has been **bo**und using handcraft methods **and S**myth-sewn to ensure dura**bi**li**ty**.

Photo research by **Jane** Sanders.

The dust jacket and **interior** were designed by **Corinda** Cook.

The text was **compiled** and edited by Susan **K.** Hom.

The text was set in **Aveni**r, Cascade Script, Forte, Impact, **M**onotype Sorts, Sho Roman, **Script**, Southwest Ornament, and Univers.